AFRIKA CRYISIS

Africa Crisis

By

DELUKE MUWANIGWA

COPYRIGHT @ 2021 AFRIKA CRYISIS
(Africa Crisis)
by Deluke Muwanigwa

ISBN:
Hardbound-978-621-470-000-4
Mobile/Kindle-978-621-470-001-1
Softbound-978-621-470-002-8

Published by Poetry Planet Book Publishing House
Cover photo design by Tess Ritumalta
Edited Marie Ezekiel

Photos used in the banners were taken in Pinterest and may contain their own copyrights

ACKNOWLEDGMENT

I would like to thank my indefatigable publisher, Poetry Planet Publishing House. Madam Ritumalta and her wonderful team. They have afforded me an outlet to give the world a different perspective. To all my friends who have encouraged me to write these poems.

Mister Al Gore.

PREFACE

Don't fool yourself. Africa is not a hopeless case. Africa is not a country, but a continent with fifty-four countries. The West would like to perpetuate a stereotype to justify neo-colonialism to pacify their curious people. The East is joining the racial profiling bandwagon. Both at their peril. Some Western countries leech on Africa, their survival as vibrant societies depending on Africa. No matter what propaganda and machinations are wrought upon this continent of immense beauty and resources endowment Africa will continue to rise. These poems try to give the world a small view of Africa that is buried in the cacophony of negative. Come be black with me, for me, and with me. Welcome to Mama Africa. Titambire. Svikayi zvenyu. (You are welcome!)

TABLE OF CONTENTS

JERUSAREMA CHALLENGE

There is this musical crazy
All over the world people dancing
The origins are not at all hazy
A young musician in Africa prancing
Did a song so simple to dance
Everyone dancing now in a trance
A South African young musician
Making the world dance like a magician

The world is in trouble
But this is an opportunity
Though COVID is causing rubble
Let's come together as a world community
"Forget your troubles and dance"
Bob Marley and the Wailers sang
Lets all do the JERUSAREMA JIVE
To motivate our spirits to survive

I have an idea here on PH today
Hear me out; read me out a little
"There he goes again! "some will say
This may sound useless even fickle
But I think it's a great way to commune
To have fun as a poetic community
To get to practice doing short phrases
And our poetry skills it also raises

Instead of the JERUSAREMA craze
We do the "One Two Three" phase
Poets use Deluke's template go-ahead
Put your own story in one two three instead
We get to know how to pronounce your name

Practicing rhythm and syllables in a game
Go ahead feel free anytime let's see your skill to count
on the beat to three
Let me start with my own friends for free

Name is RM Smith
Not a blacksmith
I am love-smitten
By my kittens
One two three

From down under
Lots of thunder
Lots of wonders
Goose and gander
One two three

Gotbarrier reef
Eat lots beef
Wild wild fires
Poetry desires
One two three

Something like that and all are invited
I hope you buy in I am so excited
Let's have some real fun and pun
Forget Corona poetry in the sun
So my bard friends this is an invite
To you all to do this little exercise
When you don't have inspiration
"One two three" kills your exasperation

Go try it I think its real fun
Three two and number one

In reverse just to spice things up
Let's spice things up to spice things up
One two three four five six
Seven eight nine ten eleven twelve
Enjoy yourselves forget Corona fight
One two three who gets it right?

POEM ALL MINE

Wanna say sorry
To uncle Larry
Telling my story
Three four five

I have no gun
Or knife shogun
Just my slogan
Three four five

If I irritate you
Wanna imitate you
I don't hate you
Three four five

Freedom of speech
We can teach
Not to preach
Three four five

Right to offend
Make amends
To my friends
Three four five

Project not taken
Resolve not shaken
Spirit all waken
Three four five

I wanna stop now
Don't know how

13

I take a bow
Three four five

One two three
Four five six
Seven eight nine
Poem all mine.

I take a bow
Three four five

One two three
Four five six
Seven eight nine

333

Three hundred and thirty-three. Tonight this magic number would be fulfilled. This important number was upper most in his mind, already etched in his empty soul. Mood foul. There will be a full moon tonight, the night everything is just right for the deed to be done. But, first, he needs companionship.

Today he will be well dressed in a black tuxedo and a golden chain with a crucifix adorning his masculine herculean neck. A woman's dream of pure manliness. Handsome. Last night he was practicing to chat up a lady, a virgin, in the heart-shaped mirror where only he could view himself. Any observer behind him would see a blank mirror because there is always pitch darkness in the room.

In the evening, he will visit local pubs, parties, and any place he can hook up a date. He will mesmerize the virgin with pure charm, hypnotize her with his retina-less eyes. The girl must be exquisite. The girl must be nubile. The girl must be ready. Ready to spend the night of her hypnotized free will. At the strike of midnight after the girl is tranced from copious drafts of her choice beverage, he will complete the transformation. The most handsome werewolf the moon has ever seen.

He will sink his teeth in her neck, raise his wolf head towards the full moon, and howl into the still night. The hills in the distance will echo with a different timbre of howlers from different shrines. Tonight he will complete his sojourn to nether firmaments to live with 666 followers.333 virgins and 333 men.

He will dissolve the virgin's body in oleum and disappear into the valley to join his subjects, never to be seen again. Assignment complete.

He woke up at 3: 33pm suffering a split headache from the spirits he drank the previous night. His blood was near rupture capacity. Thank God it was just a dream!

A BLACKMAN WITH A WHITE BEARD.

There was once a black man with a white beard
He always thought people treated him a bit weird
Was it the colour of his skin?
Perhaps his thick lips were the thing?
Just when he thought all people were the same
He found some he couldn't blame.
There was once a black man with a white beard.
He found the world is not what he feared.
Wonderful people in all corners of the world
Some even kind enough to say a good word.
Some loved his white beard and black skin.
Others loved him.
There was once a black man with a white beard.
A black man with a white beard.

A HOME AWAY FROM HOME

The black person needs respite
He suffered through slavery
He suffers evil mercenaries
He suffers in his home land

The discrimination is pervasive
A black person works twice as much
A black person gets less reward
A black person lives in bondage

But, I know there is a place for Africans
I know there is a place for black people
Home from our African home
A home far away from our home

AFRICA, OUR HOME

It's amazing how much ignorance and stereotyping there is even in these days of Google and the internet. There are some who still believe Africa is still burdened by tribal wars. All it takes is to google and find out. I rather suspect, for some, there is a need to have a racial scapegoat. Someone you must necessarily feel superior to validate your own worth. Without someone to look down upon, there is an inherent feeling of worthlessness. In the meantime, time marches on relentlessly.

Africa, the proverbial dark continent, is rising and with it the lives of a billion people. No longer can other races carve up Africa into arbitrary nations as happened in Berlin in the late nineteenth century. Africa has to be consulted. Africa's voice must be heard. Black people have developed a persona as a distinctly opinionated conglomeration of distinct tribes and unique individuals.

Of course, as one threat fades others remain. We are the richest, fastest-growing and youngest population. Without Africa, some imperial countries would collapse. The exploitative relationship is slowly unravelling and machinations such as in the Ivory Coast and Haiti, are coming to naught.

China and the United States are emerging as our worst threats. Each wants to loot the resources of Africa without paying fair value and is willing to flex their military muscles.

The United States must stop pretending they are Africa's Uncle Sam benefactor. If they can't respect the sanctity of the lives of Negroes on home soil how do they expect to respect native Africans.

The history of the United States in the last 250 odd years does not inspire confidence. The unnecessary wars, the concocted reasons for invasions. Thank you for creating the World Wide Web. Information is there tucked away in the propaganda.

And, then China. It's amazing how people forget history easily. Were they not oppressed by the Japanese not long ago? Why would they want to ridicule and oppress people based on their colour and ethnicity?

A BLACK DAY

Today was one of those black days
Got home in pitch blackness
Welcomed by a power blackout
The food I forgot on the stove had burnt black
I groped in the dark so black
Could not find the knob to my black door
And dropped my Blackberry black phone in the black night.
The bed I missed bedsheets being black
In the darkness so black
Having taken some Carling Black Label
And Johnnie Walker Red Label mixed with Black
I collapsed on my black leather sofa
And blacked out
A black day.
ABD

ADAM AND EVE

"Do not ye judge so that ye may not be judged"
But you judge
It's been said
Heed never paid
Like you are afraid
Someone has strayed

Like you have a grudge
You adjudge
You are the standard
Everyone else is stranded
On this earth
Like you know why they were birthed

The animal on the farm
You shoot with a firearm
The man in the street you scorn
You deny him corn
Like in "Animal Farm"
You wish man and animal harm
Man and animal on the farm
Manimal harm

Some people are more equal than others
Have you considered their mothers
May have had a genetic mutation
Or father lived in a place with a pollution reputation
A child can be a boy-girl or a girl-girl
A girl boy or a boy boy
All combinations and permutations
You view them with perturbations

Someone's sexual orientation is private
Just like with primates
So what's it to you
If you find out someone new
Has different preferences
And you refuse to give references
Due to prejudices
Like everything sub judice

You forget the statement
Not to judge
Judge not
So you may not be judged.
Live and let live
Like Adam and Eve

AFRICA SMILE

All "Africans"

All "Africans" crossed great oceans
New complexion now treat home with caution
What goes around
Can run aground
Africa shall give the magic portion

Africa Smile

They say we live on a dark continent

They say if they give us aid

This will fulfill our contentment

Instead, they give us aid laced with AIDS

They want to wipe us out

They want to take our resources for free

Come and bask in our sunshine throughout

Don't worry my brethren shout this poem from every tree

Africa smile. Let there be no fear

Smile and overcome their prejudices

Let your thick lips stretch from ear to ear

Smile and conquer their sick injustices

They spread propaganda on CNN

Cause one brother to fight another

Give negative publicity to achieve their end

Bribe your brother to side with them rather

Rather than to see the wood from the tree

And accept only the message so free

Be able to tell the good from the bad

Let us recite this poem and make them mad

Africa smile. Let there be no fear

Smile and overcome their prejudices

Let your thick lips stretch from ear to ear

Smile and conquer their sick injustices

POEMYELITIS?

Everything I touch turns into a poem
That's a good thing
Right?
Like spontaneous combustion
It just happens

In my sleep
When I weep
In the bush
In the house

That's a good thing
Right?
After a fight
In darkness or light

In sadness
In happiness
That's a good thing
Right?

Don't know what this is
Perhaps a disease?
Poemyelitis?
Poemyelitis

STOP OBJECTIFYING

Just as there are those with blonde hair
Just as there are those with skin dark or fair
Those that are tall
And those in between not short at all

The colour of a person's skin is not a reflection of
personality
A mirror of capability
Stop stereotyping
Stop objectifying

Just as some people are, not by choice, women
Some are born men, praise the Lord, Amen
There are women preferring to be male
Men having feelings of being a female

The appearance of a person's face is not a reflection of
personality
A mirror of capability
Stop stereotyping
Stop objectifying

Whether you are "Black or White"
Whether your name is "Billie Jean"
You prefer to "Keep it in the closet"
Or prefer the "Man in the mirror"
"We are the world"
Let's spread the word

The colour of a person's skin is not a reflection of
personality
A mirror of capability

Stop that stereotyping
Stop objectifying.

FAIR?

29

No one plays fair at the fair
Most carrying noses in the air
Pretending to compete
Making sure their advantage is complete
There is doublespeak
People talk and squeak
Never walk the talk
Cheating other folks
Only asking for fairness
With eagerness
When losing.

The mythical blindfolded woman
Carrying scales for all humans
Looks impressive on statues
Giving weight to statutes
Watch how the poor are robbed
Even de-robed
The colour of your skin
Deciding who wins
Money talking
Evil walking
Free

Spare me the hot air on what's fair
Let's meet at the trade fair
A pair
Play fair
Fair fair
Fair?

THE HOUSE OF STONE

My home is a solid rock
Granitic in its splendour
My people play with tinder
Believing it inflammable
Consort with frenemies
To bring our home down
For filthy lucre

I have spoken hoarsely
No one hears my soliloquy
That, no matter the sky falls
No matter rivers run dry
And promises of a good life
Home is our refuge
Umbilical cord cast in stone

I am not wanted on the scene
Kindred selling birthright
But, I shall not leave, but live here
Die here
Reincarnate here
Home of my progenitor
The house of stone.

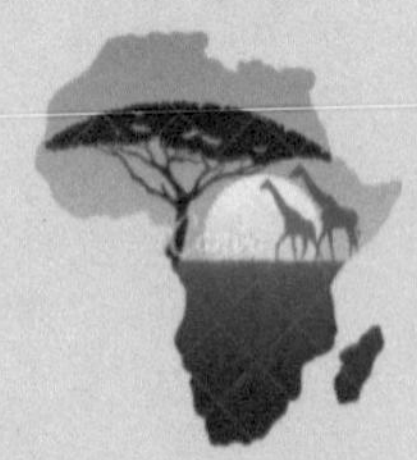

AFRICA SMILE (Acrostic)

A-ll the things we read about Africa are untrue

F-or instance fewer and fewer countries are poor

R-emaining ones are making good progress

I-ntra trade is growing with economic blocks.

C-ivil wars are a thing of the past in most

A-frican Union is becoming more relevant

S-mall businesses are supporting economies

M-en and women becoming equally empowered

I-llegal mercenary activities becoming less prevalent

L-and returning to indigenes despite foreign resistance

E-nd of the day things are looking good; so Africa Smile.

AFRICA VS. WORLD

The whole world held its breath
Covid had landed on the African coast
That continent with little to no bread,
Was not, nay, is never prepared for the cost
Graphs were plotted
Funds by WHO allotted
Very few original Africans died
Instead of celebrating haters cried

The whole world was still in shock
Scrambling for religious explanations
To understand why so few have croaked
Some say "poverty! "; with false exclamations
Some say its the young population
Graphs have been hidden,
by disappointed heathens
Wanted to make a profit from Africa's misery
As usual, peddling falsehoods for usury

We say to the world we Africans are with you
In your suffering and the thousands of dead
One thing this disease has shown as true
Is that we are all children of the Most High The Dread
"Africa smile. Let there be no fear"
"Smile and conquer sick injustices"
"Let your thick stretch from ear to ear"
"Smile and overcome their prejudices"

AFRIKA!

Went round to Westgate Shopping Centre
Grudgingly to deposit money back to the sender
The crooked banker capitalist tycoons
Ripping your life savings like a typhoon
I parked my little Fit Honda Jazz,
Walked to the bank entrance unfazed

A big burly bully guard shook his head,
pointing at his chin. "No entry! ", he said
Bollicks! I had forgotten my face mask
"Can I use the lapel of my tee-shirt? ", I asked
Goliath shook his head, hand on baton stick
Said I was adding on to people getting sick
I went to a flea market to buy a face contraption
And was allowed in by BBBG without interruption.

Our first Covid wave killed about two hundred.
Most came with the disease from overseas to see
kindred
Some already dying with terminal diseases
People here are relaxed scoffing at rules with teases
So even Engineer DM with all his supposed education
left home without a mask and with BBBG had an
altercation.

They say a second wave is definitely coming
We are still waiting for the first wave running
There is a scientific reason why we Negros in Africa
weathered the storm better than people in Antarctica
Scientists are baffled, haters and racists disappointed
Whatever it is this time around we are the chosen race,
anointed

God is great Africa!
Allahu akbar Afrika!

God is great Africa!
Allahu akbar Afrika!

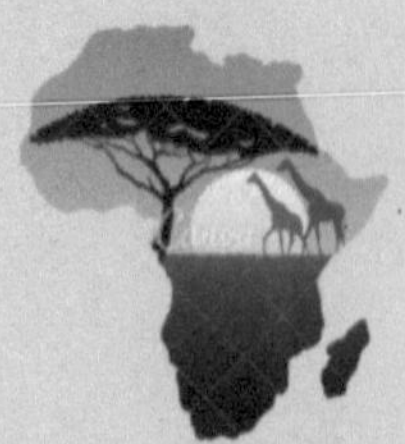

ALL LIVES MATTER

All lives matter
What you did not create
Do not render asunder

All lives matter
What you cause a threat
God strikes you with thunder

All lives matter
What you have met
God loves even down under

All lives matter
What you can bet
Take your 666 number

Don't take His position
And end another's life
Because All Lives Matter

AN ALIEN

Ellen saw an alien in the alley
She felt sorry fed him the bread of barley
A poor immigrant
Said his name was Grant
Ellen's home became the best in the valley

An alien

A strange-looking man called out to Ellen
Hiding in the alley from Homeland Security covered in
Pollen
She felt sorry for him took him home to feed
Told the police they must check the alley in the morning
instead

An alien

A-ll people on earth are aliens
N otwithstanding your origin
A-ll of us came into this world
L-ive well wherever you are
I-nfact we all came from somewhere
E-nforcing a ban on immigration
N-egates the philosophy of creation

APOLOJERSEY

So it came to pass during our coup, not a coup
Itself quite a breakthrough
A youth leader wrote scathing remarks about the
conspirators
Naivete made him not know the coup had collaborators
When the puschs dust settled he was detained
At the point of detente

He was made to read his communique
When he finished they clapped hands and ordered him
to read again his communication
The youth leader wore a checkered
 jersey
In Zimbabwe, the jersey has become a symbol of
apology
If you've done something wrong and you ask for
forgiveness they ask
"Where is your apolojersey? "

An apology requires an apolojersey

BLACK SON

Blacks lack the tack to attack their slackness
Relying solely on their blackness
God gave everything
They lack in nothing
Bowl and bench made of gold is not lackness

Black Son

Africa is a very rich place
God gave to the black race
There are those who covet
try to use methods covert
To loot Africa's resources
To stunt its peoples' life sources
God gave black people their udder
But some do deals with a hand under
With blunted consciences
With hellish consequences

Those who doubt Africa's Statistics
This is not a propaganda tactic
2020 Population 1.3 billion
2050 Population 2.2 billion

Now 55 African States
Now 17% world population
Now 90% platinum supply
Now 90% of cobalt supply
Now 75% of coltan supply
Now 50% gold supply
Now 66% of manganese supply
Now 35% uranium supply

Now 9.6% of oil production

Impressive all-around numbers
Africa, what is it that encumbers,
your children to eat in large numbers? RELIGION lulls
you into a slumber,

Do you believe in God?
Are churches after gold?
If you truly believe in God
Do you obey His code?
Do you think the real God
Is the one in scripture told?
Do you believe the real God
Would allow the human folk
To tamper with his human flock?
So, do you believe the real God
Is the one people are told?
Do you believe everything sold?
Your short life rendered cold
Do you also want some gold?
But pray to a humanoid god
While people loot your gold?
Do you believe in gold?
Do you believe in God?

If you answer without fear, favor, and threats,
you would walk your dark skin bright on this earth

Please My Son,
My Black Son.

THE BLACK SOUL

He does not know which process will cleanse him. He has agonized over his existence. Whether to alter his pigment like a chameleon to blend in with his immediate environment. His immediate locale is too bright for him to blend in; lit by lanterns which he designed and built during those rare moments when his overlord would refrain from chiding him with a "Youche! " Whether to use melamine sheets to conceal his coat of melamine or whether to bleach his visage and endure the caricature of a jester; he wonders. Even his soul which shown so superiorly radiant has blackened, charred by half a millennia of abject trauma; some due to self-flagellation and others due to extreme deliberate emasculation at the hands of pure evil.

Ten thousand years ago he ruled the earth. His body was a pure bundle of sinew; his powerful build he knew how to use to maximum effect. Long before his tormentor knew himself. He was so endowed with heavenly might no one dared to question his wisdom and strength; power-driven by a kinky crown perched up on his proud head adorned with thick luscious lips, a flat efficient air intake duct, and eyes so soulful you just wanted to beat the drum, stomp your feet and dance in festivity to celebrate such spendour. He ruled the earth and the earth, with its floral and fauna, bowed down in reverence. Now he wanders on the dark fringes embarrassed to show his two-tone colour visage. He is now always hiding in dark shadows, himself so black in his soul it's easy to miss him passing by.

King Phiyanki and Tahaka have been turning in their sarcophagi wondering what happened to his tribes of erstwhile powerful subjects. They were in front now they self efface. They ruled now they are ruled. They built the pyramids now survive on usury and pyramid schemes. They built the gardens of Babylon, but now even hide from papillon; scared to venture out and display their kinky hair. His womenfolk by far the most endowed female species wears mane of dead women from far off lands to self efface and fit in the foreign mould. Her precious endowments are denigrated in movies, pictures, and advertisements. Everywhere she looks, reads, and views, she is told to obey a certain chic foreign appearance which on closer inspection makes them look like masquerades. In the meantime, foreign male species are surreptitiously ogling the back, the side, form, and shape of the original human woman hiding her tantalizing sexy bode in the shadows.

But wait! Is the black phoenix rising?

There is a concerted almost involuntary reflex to keep the black soul in the dark shadows. Methods vary but the end game is the same. His genesis is a "shithole". His image is that of a murderer, a rapist, pedophile and propaganda say if he is said to be guilty he IS guilty. No need to waste taxpayer funds finding out whether the altercation is trivial or between doting friends. Quick; shoot him before he does too much damage with hands held up high or he is fleeing for his life. Can't let him go because HE will commit a crime. So send him to the shadows where his dark skin, nay, his dark soul will blend in, never to be missed. The black soul, though, will continue to rise. There is more where he from. A billion of them. The black soul.

BOGEYMAN

He makes promises at meetings
Sounding all hopeful and sweet
To the man on the street promising a treat
The bogeyman is elusive indeed

Sounding all hopeful and sweet
He drives around with a posse of armed men acting
strictly
The bogeyman is elusive indeed
If you criticize him better run away with speed

He drives around with a posse of armed men acting
strictly
To the man on the street promising a treat
If you criticize him better run away with speed
He makes promises at meetings

BUNK, BOO, PLAY TRUANT

They teach you lies, all lies, all lies
Pull wool over your eyes your eyes your eyes
They teach you western history
Treat African History like a mystery

Bunk the history lesson my friend, bunk the lecture
Black people, black children, skip the history lesson
Play truant, play truant, stop the history lesson.
Black people, black children, boo the history teacher.

Brainwash you with their nursery rhymes
Don't mention their slavery crimes
Hide the names of black inventors
Replace black inventors with impostors.

Bunk the history lesson my friend, bunk the lesson
Black people, black children, skip the history lecture
Play truant, play truant, boo the history teacher
Black people, black children boo the history teacher.

Did you know, did you know
We built the pyramids in Egypt
First in the north pole was an African
The first millionaire woman was black
First Open heart surgery by black man
The real Mc Coy was black
Train coupling systems by a black man
Truck refrigeration by a black person
Torpedo launching by a black woman
They don't say so in history books
They are liars cheats and crooks

Bunk the history lesson my friend, bunk the lesson
Black people, black children, skip the history lesson
Play truant, play truant, skip the history lesson
Black people, black children, boo the history teacher.

THE GOOD BUSINESS OF GOD

The good business of God gets sown with weeds
Everyone thinking of Him according to needs
Yet we are all blessed
Though we act all messed

Each has been given a chance to enjoy free air
To carry a beautiful piece of God's hair
God's face, His spirit, and His image
In our competition to live differences emerge

We sow hatred, discrimination, and prejudice
Drifting from Him and His privileges
The good business of God gets sown with weeds
We pay dearly for drifting from His creed.

Let's all change our wayward ways
And love each as our God says

BY ANY MEANS

I feel like riding my winnowing basket
flying in the middle of the night causing harm
I feel like riding my mystical broom stored in my casket
flying away to torment poor villagers at the farm

My heart has been turned inside out, blood flowing
outside my skin
I feel like hurting someone badly committing a sin
I feel like making progress in my life being horrible
To get what I want by any means possible

I want to really amass wealth and power
For it seems all this talk of a better life is sour
A way to lull me while the smart grab a good life by any
means
For it seems all these prayers shutting my eyes is for
people to pinch

They want to have a headstart on a good life
But I m going out there guns blazing wielding a knife
Step out of my way to see the light of day
Step up with money and riches, it's time to pay.

IF YOU SEE ME THROUGH THE COLOUR OF MY SKIN

Know that; that mirror is thin
I am not what you see
I am not my skin
I have a soul so profound it carries the earth
As I have done for years building the world with mirth
Under subjugation with bravery
Educating the world so cleverly
I gave music, still, give music
I gave love, still, give love to the sick
When next you see me be free
I am more than the colour of my skin
Love me blue black
I will love you back

DIHYDROGEN OXIDE

Enables things to grow
Including seeds you sow
This we all know
So let it freely flow
Bringing life in tow

Dam it
Damn it
Name it
Share it
Conserve it

The next war next century
With drones and cyborg centurions
Will be due to penury
Tom, Dick, and Harry fighting Henry
Over this special fluid short in the tunneling

We call it water
Is short when hotter
Some call it H2O
Chemical name is known by all
Its scientific name Dihydrogen oxide

Dihydrogen oxide
Store it inside and outside
The cliche water is life
Distill water you get oxygen for life
Hydrogen for fuel cells with long life

Dihydrogen oxide
Union of two hydrogens one oxygen

Two husbands with one wife
To support all life
Soon we will search for it with a knife

Water
Dihydrogen oxide
H2O
Damn it
Dam it

Two husbands with one wife
To support all life

UNCLE TOM MEANT

Do you know what torment is?

Torment is when uncle Tom decides to hate you
Torment is when uncle Tom meant to kill you

Do you know what torment is?

Torment is when uncle Tom tries to burn you
Torment is when uncle Tom meant to poison you

Do you know what torment is?

Torment is when uncle Tom becomes uncle Sam
Tom meant is when uncle Tom meant to be uncle Sam.

Do you know what torment is?

Torment is when uncle Sam meant to invade you
Torment is when uncle Tom becomes uncle Sam

Do you know what torment is?

Torment is when uncle Tom knew uncle Sam wants to
destroy you
Tom meant uncle Sam is coming to dominate you

Do you know what torment is?

Torment is when uncle Sam does what he, please
Torment is when uncle Sam spreads the disease.

Do you know what torment is?

Do you know what?
Do you know?
Do you?

DIG!

I laugh I love I loaf
I need to eat a loaf
Loaf of bread is never free
Sometimes the bread is tree
Or in the soil on surface
Or deep in-ground furnace
You drink your sweat
You gulp it wet
No matter how hard
To have bread with lard

Get digging digging digging
Get digging digging digging
Digging digging digging
Digging digging digging

If you eat a treat while you sit still
Then you steal someone else fill

Thief!
Thief!

You live the life of a lurch
You ought to go to church
Ask for divine forgiveness
Of God, His Holiness
Then do the confessional
Promise to a professional
Gather your wits
Go on the street
Get a job
Like Job

Get digging digging digging
Get digging digging digging
Digging digging digging
Digging digging digging

Get digging
Digging
Dig!

DOWN WITH RACISM (Acrostic)

Do you know science proves everyone came from Africa
Over there, where you are, you are my descendant
Where, then, do you get the temerity to hate me,
therefore yourself
New variations of colour all came from me, the Negro

White, yellow, red, orange, and everything in between
In case you doubt do research on where all humans
began
The trouble is the factional politics of religion
How it creates stories to control our minds to suit some

Regardless of what science, the real religion which
works, says
And, if you doubt science, put a polythene bag over
your head
Crash your head on a rotating guillotine
Ingest cyanide, antifreeze, and see if you can pray to
save yourself
So, my children, my descendants, my people, let's love
one another
My message to you is; Down with racism.

DON'T STOP

At the end is a new beginning
On the way you find are other ways
Everything seems to change to remain the same anyway
Acceptance includes non-acceptance
Inductance the other form of reluctance
So long as you never look the beast in the eye,
for it will absorb your spirit and soul, yes, it will try

Stand in your position and absorb your surroundings till
you become one. Defeat is a state of mind the victor in
front is behind because he won
He is already down before it's said aloud
Develop a sixth, a seventh, and as many senses as your
life force allow

Spend time on your own in the forest standing still for
hours
Those who observe will understand you are not a
coward
Sitting by a stream bank watching the water cascading
down
will infuse music of the stream you won't frown.

The difficult and the easy incline each other.
A difficult situation is a small bother
If there is life there is hope
If there is a will there is scope
You will cope
Carry on

Don't stop
Used?... if so ignore it

DREAMS OF FREEDOM

You can chain me in a dungeon
My God-given freedom you bludgeon
But even as i rot in positional gangrene
Even as my circulating blood congeals
The atoms and molecules in me vibrate
You cannot stop freedom to happen, magistrate!
Even if I die in your political prison
My soul and spirit freely leaves on

When you curtail my ideas my dissent
You imprison yourself in a rut so indecent
A part of you has to commit to lying and propaganda
To justify why I am in prison in your jail but never in
Uganda
We are together in your penitentiary
You act free but your degrees of freedom is curtailed
exponentially
Mr leader Mr implied prisoner your freedom to rule
Derives from freeing yourself by freeing the fugitive.

We all have dreams of freedom
In all our kingdoms
We dream of freedom
Dreams of freedom

ENCORE! ENCORE!

I'm tired of pretending I am alive when I m dead
People seeing a hologram of me instead
Carrion has cleaned my inside and outside
My form and figure bereft of existence outright
All my history and memory embedded in invisible bones
I wander around, you think you see me, but I'm gone

What you see is not there
These are illusions
These are delusions
What you see is not fair

How can I exist without a home?
How can I exist without a form?
How can I exist without a name?
How can I exist without my game?
How can I exist without a country?
How can I exist without a pantry?
How can I exist without my garb?
How can I exist without my farm?
How can I exist without a totem?
How can I exist without them?

Maiweeee! Yohweeee!

They bombed my village
They went on a pillage
They colonized me
Then, they said I m free
They took my land
They killed my eland
They banned my shrine

Then, called it a crime

Gods of our land, guardians of our totem, hear our
pleas!
Help us reach the Creator of all man and plead for us,
please!
Mbuya Nehanda you are letting us down!
Sekuru Kaguvi, fire is burning us to the ground!

We went, we fought, we died and cried
We killed, we freed, we triumphed they fled
Instead of my apparition in flesh and blood appearing
Instead of going back to the glorious days, I m fearing
Our people will have to recite this poem again, Encore!
People read this poem from the first line, Encore!

Encore! Encore!
Encore! Encore!

EQUAL

Give me an equal fight
Equal right
Equal rice

Give me equal seed
Equal feed
Equal need

Give me equal oil
Equal soil
Equal toil

Give me equal race
Equal space
Equal pace

Give me an equal vote
Equal note
Equal home

Give me equal equal
Equal equal
Equal

EVERY

For years I blamed my mum
For leaving me when I was young
What I did not understand
There was a plan so grand

Now I have come of age
I have reached the crucial stage
What I thought important in life
Now I just take in my stride

Even if my children disowned me now
I would just wipe the sweat off my brow
And carry on living till my last day
I'd be sad but have not much to say

If my wife of decades decided to leave
I would brood but continue to live
For I know I will never be alone
God provides me a permanent home

Every child is my child
Every bride my bride
Every mother my mother
Every man my brother

As long as you are living
To you love I will be giving
I will share the little I have
This is how we should behave

EVERY ONE DIES

Congratulations whoever or whatever will kill me
Big kudos from me
I have been there, done that
Any challenge, my retort, 'So what? '

There comes a time for retrogression
When you have no appetite for progression
Aggression
And possessions

You lay down
Dressed in your gown
Maggots do their work
Decompose your world
Back to nature
No more stature
Fist clenched over your chest
Last fist pump before your rest

Satisfied
Stratified
You lie on top of the swastika
Enemies of Afrika

Despite their lies
Every one dies
Those who labeled you backward
You lie on top of them in your graveyard

EXEUNT

If you tickle me I laugh
If attracted I love
You prick I bleed
I run with speed
When I am afraid
I am human bred

I see so much aloofness
In humans a goofiness
Like when we expire
When we finally retire
We carry our attitude
To an unknown latitude

In the twenty-first century
Some live in penury
Others do not want
Abundance their grant
There's no sympathy
There's no empathy

Many in misunderstanding
Charlatans grandstanding
Pretending to know
People still fall
Dying alone
Still like a stone

Some play Him Judge
Your mind they nudge
From their fictional point of view
Saying nothing new

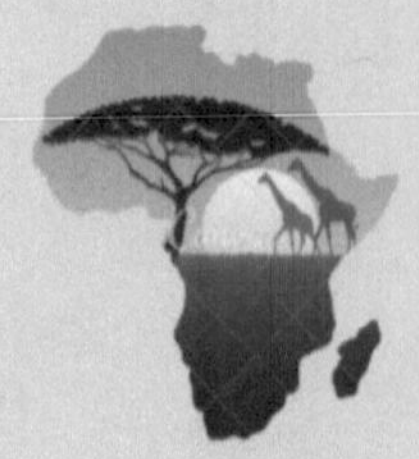

They want your soul
Intention most foul

It is obvious
But to some oblivious
The world community
Has autonomy and immunity
Soon you die alone
So beware of the con

No matter what you say
No matter on which day
Deluke will have a look
At the gook de gook
To the subtle effluent
And bow exeunt

FATHER KNOWS

Looked to my spouse
She was down and out
Knew not who she was
She could've been me
My daughter
Our son
Mary the Virgin
Or no one at all
I mothered my daughter
Got her a toy
Fathered my boy
Got muted approval

Father knows what to do

My inlaws the outlaws
Siblings skeptical
I must have done it
Must have caused it
The meltdown
The regression
Must be my fault
My stepmom said
"Son, hang in there"
"This is your moment"
"Forget the comments"
"Do what your father would"

Father knows what to do

Arms akimbo
Exuding confidence

My insides boiling
Numb from head to toe
Fear of the dark
Vacuum in my head
Not sure what to do
Kids spoke with their eyes
I, hiding my butterflies
pretending

Father knows what to do

Lonely in the crowd
At the crossroads
Decision by instinct
Wife's job terminated
Kids school uprooted
Money stuffed in a jacket
Property in removals
No time for goodbyes
Crossed the frontier
Leaving the good life
Journeyed all night
For better for worse

Father knows what to do

FEAR OF THE DARK!

Is there a specialist out there?
Someone to treat Western phobias?
Is there a remedy for this condition?
Someone, to calm their fears?

They don't have agoraphobia
Nor arachnophobia
They have Claustrophobia
They have something worse
They fear fear fear those who are dark
Fear of the dark fear of the dark fear of the DARK!

They spend millions saying they superior
But they discriminate they won't compete
They try to exterminate black people
They try to wipe out their fear

They don't have agoraphobia
Nor arachnophobia
They have claustrophobia
They have something worse
They fear fear fear those who are dark
Fear of the dark fear of the dark fear of the DARK!

Don't they realize it's just a skin
Don't they realize it's so thin
Don't they realize it's just a pigment
Their fear a figment

They don't have agoraphobia
Nor arachnophobia
They don't have claustrophobia

They have something worse
They fear fear fear those who are dark
Fear of the dark fear of the dark fear of the DARK!

FISH OUT OF WATER

I am fish out of water. My gills are running out of life-giving water. My scales are peeling off little by little. I am trying to close my eyes, but I was never endowed with eyelids.

I reminisce about the good old days in the sea swimming among the sharks. It was dangerous, but at least we could hide in the corals and wait for the sharks to swim by. The lionfish we could spot even in the dark. We were much safer.

I remember migrating to freshwater channels but we started injesting plastic pellets. We don't know where these came from. There were dangerous nylon strings with a shiny piece of metal with tantalizing worms gyrating rhythmically in the tide.

Many of my brothers and sisters got hooked and got yanked out of the water by this dangerous predator. This predator I could see shape-shifting above water, sometimes on the bank or sometimes sitting in an odd-shaped fiberglass raft.

I do not have much time left so let me say my prayers. My totem is the fish. All living things were derived from me, adapting from the deep sea in search of better homes away from whales, sharks and dolphins. Some of those creatures now turn against me and out of cannibalism have developed a taste for me.

Anyway, I see a stream of water not far. If I can just wriggle a little I might just fall in. If I make it you will hear from me. If I don't make it you will not hear from me.

My last words will be, " I can't breathe! ".

FROM DUST TO DUST

I came from dust
I belong to dust
From it, I was fashioned by hand,
my roots radiating from the land.

If you take away my land,
I cannot stand it.
I cannot grow at all,
you cause me to fall

Which fool gives up his soil,
native resentment on the boil.
Creating danger for anger,
placating the evil stranger

I'm not a terrorist when I explode,
you caused my life to implode.
It's my homeland or bust.
From dust to dust.

FULL OF IT

Friends don't worry about me
Just my humor my spirit is free
Enemies, I do sleep in a casket
I travel at night in a winnowing basket
You see I am in Africa Africa
Different than South Africa
Here we do serious voodoo
The voodoo we do do
And of course, if you believe
I will be very very relieved
I would have influenced someone
All my life I have conned no one
I admire the sick politicians
Conjuring up fiction like magicians
The so-called Men of God
Extorting money and gold
So if you believe I fly high in a basket
at night sleep in a reed casket
You need a gasket check, brain surgery
Your brain scanned for the injury
I am just a simple guy full of it
Enjoy your day at night don't look for it
The reed basket
Nor the casket

FUTURE IN SUTURE

Truth hurts but without it, nothing is solved
All the same from the truth we are not absolved
We cannot fix our problems by false pretense
That by sticking band-aids we get competence
Everything about our governance is wrong
We pretend our economy will be strong
They say by twenty-thirty we will be middle income
But our wasteful consumption is burdensome

I hope there will come a time when truth be told
The whole truth whether hot or cold
A time when we will rewrite everything in our
constitution
A time we will hold all people equal and accountable
with restitution
A time where entitlement as a result of history
Is banished abolished never to be evoked causing
misery
For now and for the foreseeable unfortunate future
As people, we limp on in delusions and brinkmanship in
sutures

GAME OF EARTH

People are still preparing for war
Preparing to defend their corner of the world
Preparing to wrought pain and woe
As if accommodation and talking ever failed
Yet we are all temporary eaters of the pie
We are born, we thrive briefly and die
Where is the love commanded?
Go forth and multiply as demanded?
By the one who created everything
The one power we feel but never see

Let us universally renounce religion
Psychologists hacking our minds
Therein lie conflicts based on regions
With stories so fantastic yet so behind
And expend our energies on science
We will destroy our world with silence
Not speaking about the dangers of conflict
Religious wars the damage they inflict
There is enough space on earth
Disasters and pandemics regulating births

No need to fight over territory
No need to war over history
See each other in your neighbour
Help each other with ex-pat labour.
Cast away the demon called religion
One love on earth in all its regions
Stop the saber-rattling game of death
Taking territory as the Game Of Earth
Stop the Game Of Earth.
The Game Of Earth

EXEUNT

This is my refuge
No subterfuge
I want to be free
A bird in a tree
To express
And address
You don't have to agree
With my poetic pedigree
Don't control
With protocol
My thoughts
I was taught
To ask why
So why?
Why?
Sigh!

GAME PLAN

The bulb in the brain lights up
You might need coffee or tea in a cup
To get the heart pumping more blood
To get those neurons to flood

Eureka! An idea is born
But your mind is torn
One mind says don't do
The other says do you fool

You need a game plan
Do a game plan
A Game plan
Game plan

A poet may start with a title
Ideas flowing through a tight hole
Or from just a common word in the world
Do you rhyme or just have words reading weird?

What's your point of view?
Is it something totally new?
Something trite outright?
Or something slightly out of sight?

The mental video plays in your mind
Your doubt and inhibitions left behind
The poem is already done by yourself
It has, in your mind, written itself

You have a game plan
You do a game plan

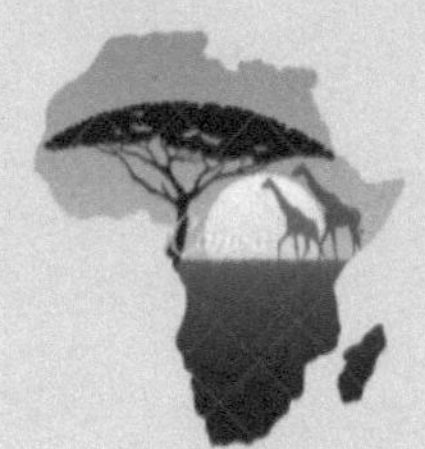

A game plan
Game plan

(CLT04052021)

Captains Log Tuesday 04052021
Coordinates from the nearest star
150.86*10 to the power of 6 km. 384.4*10 to the power
of 3kms to satellite moon. Docked on a benign
planetary system with 21 percent Oxygen. Dihydrogen
Oxide everywhere. Main life form: Semi-intelligent
humanoid.

What a busy day for a budding cosmonaut.
Berthed car ship at the nerdy humanoid auto mechanic.
Out here in the Milky Way.
To get high-tech light-emitting diode star lights
retrofitted.
Car ship Honda Fit, GD1, 2 by 4.

IN AFRICA

A pestilence persisting in three corners of the world
The dragon, breathing particulate fire
Setting fire to pharyngeal tissues
The world labouring to breathe, breeding pandemic
mania
Three corners of the world hypoxiating, the fourth
corner, mysterious as expected, breathing nonchalantly

The place of voodoo dolls, darkness, and penury.
Folklore goes, mixed with mysticism born out of
ignorance.
Images flashed on TVs, newspapers, phones, and
tablets,
of a long lost dark place of little hope, little scope for
progress
The contradiction is that the Adventists who left their
havens with scriptures are not encumbered in strictures
There is no wish to retrace their steps, preferring a life
in the lost world, the real heaven.

The usual propaganda machinery churning out
regurgitated stereotypical predictions,
"There is not enough of everything"
Medicines
Doctors
Hospitals
Only the image of the voodoo they do persists in the
minds of philanthropists.

Floodgates of sympathy opened
Foundations issue dire opinions
Graphs of morbidity plotted

Relief money allotted
A year down the pandemic
The dead are, in comparison, academic
North of Antarctica
In Africa

BILLION SHADES OF DARKNESS

Sometimes I am like an orange the skin of which is
knifed off
Other times, worse, like a lemon
Knifed, peeled, squeezed, and discarded
Exposed with the pith of my soul.
That's not all

I try to hide deep in the sea of humanity
To drown my sorrows in my pigment figments
Fishers of many hook me up to shore
De-scale, suffocate, saving me only for serving.
Serving the dinner table with my yoke of hunger.

I bleach to blend, to fit in the bright light,
wear long strands of hair of cadavers to look fair,
but still, get the feeling I am peeling under the gaze
even in a haze,
with nowhere to hide except to ride forever in billion
shades of darkness.

GOING HOME

Someone hates your personality
Two of you have no commonality
They want you to go away
Even if you want to stay
They cause a storm in your mind
Behave in many ways unkind
You have talked many a time
It's like you committed a crime
They say the room ain't big enough for both of us.
You say as you catch the next bus.

I am going home
Home where I belong
I need to sit down and think long
Sit in the garden like a gnome,
and make some resolutions
This could be a revolution
I am going, going, going home
Going, going, going home.

GOING SOUTH

You go east northwest
Seeking a different life
Speaking a different tongue
Me, I am going south

South is where my heart is
Deriving life from nature
When the journey is over
You, don't follow me south

Me, I am going south
I am going south
Past the Cape of Good Hope
To my new southern home

HAPPY HOUR

Happy hour happy hour
Happy hour I feel the power
Happy hour I am like a flower
Happy hour in my ivory tower

It is not the hour of imbibing
It is not a good wine I m describing
Or at the pub when beer is half price
Or when I am served chicken and rice

It is not when a pastor's speech touches my heart
When I understand creation from the start
When at the synagogue I am in heaven in advance
Nor the feeling of completeness God may grant

Neither is it the quality time I spend
Riding waves, taking the sharp bend
The thrill, the rush, the surge of adrenaline
All splashed up, not a care or worry for my Melanie.

My happy hour when I write a rhyme
My happy hour when I write a stanza
My happy hour when I write a verse
My happy hour when I write a POEM

That is my happy hour
My happiest happy hour

ZIMBABWE - THE HOUSE OF STONE

I look at the life of my people and see so much wastefulness and futility. If I speak out I am accused of hostility. Yet, my love for my people knows no bounds. I look around its astounding how rich, beautiful and resourceful we are but our mental slavery envelope is so thick it makes me sick. I have not met more hardworking, good-natured people like Zimbabweans.

We are a happy-go-lucky people easy-going, humour r us. We laugh all the time. Even when things are serious we find humour. We find humour at funerals, at beerhalls, in calamity, and adversity. We find humour.

The world will remember our former President, one Robert Mugabe now late, and how he would bring the house down with his humour at the United Nations. You might not like what he was saying but he would say it anyway. Tony Blair and George W. Bush were his favourite taunts...and they deserved it too.....

Zimbabwe has so much potential in terms of rich resources and human capital. The level of education was next to none...although the quality or rather the content was all colonially driven and based on not producing leaders but rather workers. As we know workers are two a penny but leaders a rare breed. Our problem stems from a lack of belief in ourselves. We want to wait for someone to lead us. Our so-called friends or benefactors be they American, Chinese, Russian, or whoever will never love us. Their coziness is exploitative. Don't be fooled Zimbabwe. Get off your ass and do it yourself. I could go on and on and on but I summarise thus

1. We should only teach STEM subjects in school

2. Religion should be diminished especially at the state level

3. Turn churches and theological facilities into technicons

4. Revamp education to produce leaders and not workers

In order to achieve this, we need freedom freedom freedom

Women must be free and equal
Youths must be free to dream their delusions because from them come innovations
LGBT must be free for we know not why they are
Meritocracy, democracy, and freedom
Ban religion in schools because it's dangerous and is an instrument of mind control and oppression

The most important issue, though is that of our land. Mugabe had his faults but on the land issue, he was spot on. We are not a people until we have a place...a real estate we can call our own. That land is Zimbabwe. Our birthright. Our Ubuntu. Our Zimbabweanness. "Our house of stone"

Land grabbers

People of Zimbabwe
People of Zimbabwe
People of Zimbabwe
We are going to find a way

All they want is perpetual subjugation
They say we are hewers of wood
It is not true don't be fooled
We are going to show this is subjective

How can forty-five hundred settlers
Own seventy percent of the soil
And make a profit from our sweat and toil
We are going to take the land and helter-skelter

They call us land grabbers
They call us to farm invaders
They say there is no rule of law
They think they make our spirits low

ZIMBABWE

1)Literacy Stats

We have the highest literacy rate
We can read better than other states
Everyone with a book
Learn to be a crook
Zimbabweans corruption we abate

2)ZIMBABWEANS (Acrostic)

Zambia is our northern Siamese twin
In the north of our teapot shaped land
Mozambique borders us to the east
Botswana is to the West of us
All these neighbours we owe gratitude
Most were affected by our bush war
Bore the brunt of cross border raids
We are grateful for feeding refugees
Even some guerrillas trained there
And, we helped liberate the next states
Namibia we freed from South Africa
South Africa from apartheid regime
Weapons of Mass Deception(WMD)

They said there are WMD
The gullible believed it
They said prisoners are POW
The fallible believed it
Every hour on BBC
Every hour on CNN
They lied even showed pictures
Breaking news canceled all fixtures

WEAPONS OF MASS DECEPTION(WMD)

Worse than weapons of mass destruction

Does the truth matter anymore
Television is a battleground
Should we trust them oh no
The rich run the world aground
We grow up hating each other
One brother fight another
There is a North-South divide
The East the West they deride

Weapons of mass deception
Worse than weapons of mass destruction

WHO is telling the truth?

Africans twice likely to experience,
COVID-19 without any illness,
WHO report said in its fullness
Unlike people of the rest of the world,
WHO analysis has unfurled

The results explain the low death rate,
confounding early results of a dire fate
in poor Africa's efforts at containment
And early predictions of devastation on the continent.

80 percent of Africans asymptomatic
Graphs plotted found to be asymmetric
50 percent rest of the world tally
Africans standing their ground totally

No health systems overwhelmed
No large cases things underwhelmed
no evidence of excess mortality
Unlike HIV not based on morality

Africa, a population of 1.2 billion,
Only about 1.4 million cases
Less than 35,000 deaths from the virus Africa unfazed,
far lower than other regions
All African people, all religions

Pundits are at pains to explain
Hiding their racist charts, they exclaim

Lower testing rates in Africa,

this fails to explain the difference between Dorica in the
US and Africa Erica
there is no miscalculation of death figures,
And the pandemic is now diminishing the reason not yet
figured
The number of new African cases has been dropping
Doomsayers scratching heads in the dark groping

They say it's because of Africa's youthful population.
They say it's why but this all futile discombobulation
3 percent of Africans are over the age of 65 they
postulate
Africa's lower population density they calculate
people who live in rural areas are freer
spending time outdoors in their career

African Governments instituted strict lockdowns
The so-called undemocratic clown's dictatorships rose
to the task
Early reaction enforced no one to counter ask

Blah blah blah blah blah blah blah
Drone waffle blah blah blah blah

Who is telling the truth? WHO

WHO PROFITS?

'Not in a thousand years will there be majority rule'
If only he knew
In sixteen years we would be free
Like a flock of ravens perched on a tree
Our white-collar bishop first to open shop
Now we say Zimbabwe is open for business non-stop
Or is it?
Who profits?

WHEN I DIE

When I die there's one tiny reason I would want to
resurrect
Failing which, as in ghost, I will insurrect
I have done fairly well in my life
With enemies, we agreed to put away the knife
With friends, I will have paid my debts
Deities I will ask for forgiveness upon death

I shall be a free soul
Destined for peaceful rest in my hole
But for this tiny bit of unfinished business
It gives me uneasiness
I may ask for reincarnation
To come back do my incartation
Or demand outright resurrection
If the gods their duty is in dereliction
I will forcibly come back as an apparition
Not the favoured option for a para- Christian

For there is a tinny winny issue
I have to come and pursue
When I die
Because I won't lie
Peacefully in my shroud
Pretending to be proud
Unless I resolve that little niggle
Then I can forever fly away like an eagle
To join my forefathers
To join my foremothers

This small issue
I will tell you when I die

It's a secret
See you when I die.

WHY?

My country is shaped like a teapot,
but, we can't afford bread and butter,
the tea leaves not to mention.

My country is sinking with minerals,
briefcases full of diamonds.
Few people wearing jewelry.

My country has good soils,
green all over with envy.
Silos filled with emptiness

My country is a precious jewel,
floating in the sea of Africa.
Homes built upon a rock

So, I don't understand.
We have the land
Not just some sand
Fertile pregnant soils
We toil on the red earth
To bring forth fruit
Grow our own food

Why are we hungry?

Make me understand
We have every mineral
Rare earth; heavy metals
Diamonds dazzling in our backyard
We dig gold with our palms
Oil part of the spoil

Uranium more than on Uranus

Why are we poor?

Explain to me
The people are educated
Tireless, hardworking
engineers aplenty,
geologists; chemists,
poets; musicians,
lawyers; beauticians

Why are people unemployed?

Zimbabwe!
Why?

WHAT HAPPENED ON THAT DAY

What I experienced was a story for another day
I cashed my cheque and drove across the border for
good
What happened on that day was no child play

I left everything behind without anything to say
I had to make sure I was on native soil soonest
What happened on that day was no child play

I am sure the robbers had guns to hunt me like prey
As I expected they followed me to the bank
What I experienced was a story for another day

Ruthless employer paid me a tidy sum for gratuity pay
We argued but he capitulated and said "See you later! "
What happened on that day was no child play

I asked a friend to stand outside the bank to survey
While I went inside the bank to cash the cheque
What I experienced was a story for another day

Thugs appeared; my friend signaled to lead them astray
I stayed long in the bank while friend harassed them
outside
What happened on that day was no child play
What I experienced was a story for another day.

WHO IS DISTURBING MY PEACE?

It's a lovely day
A good time to pray
Pray to the Most High
Pray for I and i and i
I sit in my studio dreaming
Lotsa reggae tunes are streaming
Playing somersaults in my mind
I see visions of peace to all mankind

Watch someone spoil my day
Who is gonna spoil my day
Watch someone disturb my peace
Who is disturbing my peace

The sky is blue and nice
The weather calls for a drink with ice
Ohh I am at leisure
Thinking of a reggae tune for pleasure
I see visions of Marley smiling
Peter Tosh cured of reggae myelitis
Great poets, I will be thanking
They're my inspiration for skanking

Watch someone spoil my day
Who is gonna spoil my day
Watch someone disturb my peace
Who is disturbing my peace

WALK AWAY WALK AWAY

What is pure love?
Does it cure the pain?
You helped her
Be the beauty she is
Helped her be the woman she is
Every man turning to ogle
Every woman wishing she was her
Turns on you say you're nothing

Walk away walk away
There are more African Queens
Walk away walk away
Nigeria smiles when you walk away

Who is she?
Naomi, Beyonce, or Destiny Etiko?
They are all like Eve
Always searching for the apple
If she finds one, another man
She finds her new Eden
Leaves you in purgatory
You've done your part man

Walk away walk away
There are more beautiful baes
Walk away walk away
Zimbabwe smiles when you walk away

You point a gun at your mother
A gun at your beautiful sister
A gun at your daughter
Point a gun at yourself...no no no

Walk away walk away
Your beauty is not yet born
Walk away walk away
Africa wants you to walk away
So walk away walk away

WALK TALK AND ROCK

I m just your average guy
Beat me insult me I don't cry
I only shed a tear for my lady
The one I can love steady
I am as tough as nails,
getting me down always fails
Unless you are the chosen one,
the one with whom I have fun

With her
I just wanna walk talk and rock
walk talk and rock

WALKING IN A BLIND WORLD

Walking in a blind world
People with eyes who can't see
Their range limited by assumptions
Multimedia slavery
Flashing words and pictures
Doctored reality
A comfort zone
Fiction
Friction

Is it true then reality can be made?
Like the reality of the sun
That it rises in the east
We could have called it west
The sun will still rise
Manufactured consent
A convenient way to live
Easy to accept
The truth to except

Stubborn like the sun
The truth
Send a Parker Probe
Get up real close
It's expensive
It's not easy
The luminosity opens our eyes for posterity
Regrettably, we believe someone's weird word
Walking in a blind world

WAR IS NOT BORING

War is not boring
No one can be snoring
With staccato bursts of the FN rifle
Then the famed AK47 we were baffled
Unless you were my last born five-year-old sister
She lay on the floor and slept the action missed her
We all took prone position on the ground
To avoid a high caliber stray round
Two hours of gunfire exchange
My first experience so it was strange

War is not boring
In the macabre dance someone scoring
My brother and I coming from tuckshops.
Sent to buy milk by mom we saw heavily armed soldiers
past the truck stop
Routine patrol we thought
But seconds later a battle was fought
Ran indoors and the whole family often lay on the floor
Gunfire raging for two hours no one in or out of the
door
When the AK47 answered the FN and NATO machine
gun
My niece stood up to ululate like she was having fun

War is not boring
In the carnage, there is no glory
The next morning we went to the scene
Mounds and mounds of cartridges to be seen
Blood was strewn all over of departed soldier souls
Bullet holes and damage to residential walls
A stray bullet struck a drunken imbiber on his bed

Seven soldiers of many ranks including a Colonel dead
Zimbabwe we must fight never again
War is not boring is still my refrain

WE

We drive in the yellow line
Against traffic any time
We drive through roadblocks
at any speed round the clock
Handguns fitted with mufflers
We are insured by the mafia
You hit me
You hit we

Rules are for fools
Rules not cool
Traffic cops know us
even the driver of the bus
The mayor's office we pay
To let us go free any day
You hit me
You hit we

We are professional jailbreakers
In our employ lawmakers
Right up to the highest office
So shut your facial orifice
the national police chief
was our best thief
You hit me.
You hit we

I am insured by the mafia

There is no one we fear
You hit me
We hit you
You hit me
You hit we

WAKE UP

Take our land (we allow them to)
Treat you bad(we allow them to)
Divide and rule(we allow them to)
Deride and fool(we allow them to)

They slap our face (we allow them to)
They insult our race(we allow them to)
It's our fault it's our fault(we allow them to)
Our arms we fold (we allow them to)

Wake up NegroMan(wake up, wake up)
Wake up BlackMan (wake up)
Wake up wake up wake up wake up wake up wake up
wake up
Wake up wake up wake up wake up wake up

VIDEO GAMES

I play video games in my mind
You play video games in your mind
We all play video games in our minds
Stop playing video games in your mind.

Wife, when your husband comes home late
Don't play video games; wait till eight
before you phone your mother-in-law
before you let the police know

Husband, when your bank account is depleted
Don't play video games; see if the new dress is pleated,
before you find a money blocking trick,
and make your wife mentally sick.

Son, when your parents say you're grounded
Don't play video games; your reason unfounded
Before you become a rebel without a cause
know that love is their reason; their because

And you, my daughter; if you stay out late
Don't play video games; lock yourself in your room
Before you become an impossible brat
mom and dad, for the same reason, have a spat

And for you; cat and dog; my favorite pets
Don't play pet video games and go on strike
Before you go letting the robber and the mouse
through,
do remember times are hard; its true

UNSHAKABLE

At daybreak I expected the sun to rise
I was in for a surprise
There was an eclipse of the sun
Like on this day the end was nigh
The sun flipped over its rays shining into the cosmos
bright
On a clear cloudless day, it was quite a sight

The moon that night is light so hot
The stars in constellation consternation they brought
The ground I stood on transparent
Making volcanic eruptions at the earth's core apparent
The stationary wind smelling of incense
Everything not making sense

I stood in wonderment
Like an explorer in a wonderland
Making the first contact
My soul intact
All my vital signs standard
Never feeling stranded

Unshakable

108

TRUTH HURTS

It hurts to tell the truth for your own truce
You saw the liberation war raging
Countrymen behaving uncouth

Countrymen behaving uncouth
Your house marked for bombing
Enemies pretending it was unused

It hurts, to tell the truth for your own truce
Even the regime BSAP got wind of this
Guarded your house the night through

It hurts, to tell the truth for your own truce
Your brother slept on the roof
The second night the BSAP withdrew

Countrymen behaving uncouth
Your independence is underwritten in blood
Many died for the freedom of your youth

Years after the war you go full circle like fools
Freedom fighters having forgotten the ethos
Countrymen behaving uncouth
It hurts to tell the truth for your own truce

I REST MY CASE

Freedom of expression is conditional upon consummating your ideas with those of the standards. Whose standards? The way it's been done always. What the whole world has accepted as a fact. A fact based on empiricism or based on imperialism?

Let's take the fact to the lab and have it certified free of emotion or conjecture or belief or faith. No. These things cannot be done in the laboratory. You must just justly verily have faith. Ummm, what if there is irrefutable empirical evidence that it is because of this lack of query and inquiry that has led to fanatical genocides and conflicts among the same people based on doctored documents politicized to suit a particular narrative as we have seen MSM do? We must still accept because everyone accepts. No!

The reason why nature gave me a medulla oblongata is so I reason, I think, to save myself and my environment and all those things in earth's firmament. It would be a dereliction of my natural duty to accept every truism in life without interrogation because that's how things are. Truth is not afraid of interrogation and criticism because it does not change. After all the trials, tribulations, and rigorous exhaustive assessment, the truth remains because it IS. It doesn't matter if one person or two billion people believe in the truth. It will be what it IS.

I rest my case.

TRUE STORY

True story, in nineteen seventy-seven I rode a pontoon
We slept on the bank of the Zambezi River in
Livingstone, Zambia
Found border closed and donated blood to vampire
mosquitoes
I was thirteen and thought we were going to sink in the
Zambezi River

We slept on the bank of the Zambezi River in
Livingstone, Zambia
We wanted to cross into Rhodesia, now Zimbabwe, our
native home
I was thirteen and thought we were going to sink in the
Zambezi River
The Rhodesian war prevented us from crossing directly

We wanted to cross into Rhodesia now, Zimbabwe, our
native home
The pontoon was filled to capacity and I could run my
toes in the water
The Rhodesian war prevented us from crossing directly
Scary hippos eyed us sailing to the Botswana border
where we crossed.

True story, in nineteen seventy-seven I rode a pontoon
If I had been a poet then I would have written a
pantoum
Scary hippos eyeing me sailing on the pontoon
Rhodesian war prevented us from crossing using
platoons

TRUE LEADERSHIP

A leader is not a manager
Neither is a manager a leader
Who the cap fits wear it
Make sure it does fit
Otherwise its a disaster
A ship without its master

Some leaders think they manage
The whole system they savage
Some managers think they lead
The whole system they mislead
A square peg in a round hole
A system taking an enormous toll

A leader is a dreamer a schemer
A manager is a filer a piler
A leader sees outcomes in deja vu
A manager sees outcomes through
Both are essential cogs
To ensure the system doesn't clog.

So shall it be
So it is
Leaders lead managers to manage
We need good managers
And true leaders in leadership
True leadership

TILL I DIE

I'm gonna sing my songs, sing my songs
I'm gonna write the wrongs, right the wrongs
I'm gonna keep chanting down Babylon
I'm gonna fight fight fight the racist Babylon

I'm gonna recite my poems of freedom
I'm gonna free the African Kingdom
Recite my poetry till I die.
Till I die, till I die, till I die

No amount of fear will stop me
I'm gonna recite it till we free, free, free
It's gonna be rhyming with fire, yeah
You can't make me feel tired, to feel tired

I'm gonna recite my poems of freedom
I'm gonna free the African Kingdom
Recite my poetry till I die
Till I die, till I die, till I die

Till I die, till I die, till I die
Till I die, till I die, tillI I die
Till I die, till I die, till I die

Till I die, Till I die
Till I die, Till I die
Till I die, Till I die

Till I die
Till i die
Till I die

I die
I die
I die.

Die
Die
Die

I die
I die

TILL KINGDOM COME

Evangelicals spoke
Giving false predictions in political talk
Lying to gullible people
Those whose minds are fickle
That God had spoken
But the vision was broken
Nothing came to pass
What a fuss
Liars!
Village criers!
God speaks to no mortal
No matter the portal.

Even then every Sunday
People troop to pray
Led by the same sages
Spreading false messages
How fickle can we be?
What will it take to see?
You can hate me
I beg you to see
God is not among the men of cloth
Full of deception, greed, and sloth
God is love
I say this till kingdom come.

TIME

Writer's block

1.

Deluke wants to write a poem today
Alas, he has very little to say
Every rhyme he musters
Disappears faster
Deluke has given up, gone out to pray

2.

Just in time

They say don't worry this is writer's block
I say no I need a poem by the clock
Got nothing to write
Because I am bright
I wrote some limerick on a cloth

Time

There is a concept severally understood called time.

Every race has its own concept of this elusive time

The Japanese believe and do things just in time,

even commit hara-kiri for failing to control time.

The West controls what it believes might is right all the
time.

116

The Chinese will do stuff slowly bide their time,

over thousands of years, they watch the unfolding time.

The most interesting slave masters of time,

are the Africans and their disregard of time.

Africans will get around to doing something sometime.

What use is it to control something as misunderstood as time?

Africa has everything it needs all the time.

Land, minerals, and everything people need especially time.

Time will tell whether African Wisdom will stand the test time.

TIME MOVES ON

I used to do one-eighty degree splits
One finger push-ups
A practioner of Jeet Kune Do
One of the best
Even defeated a Brown belt
Had my own students
Now it's just a daydream
Time moves on in days

I used to be a young engineer
Designing electrical systems
To schools, churches, clubs
Even highrise buildings with lifts
Always willing to challenge the best
Now I am connected to the earth
driving to my farm every weekend
Time moves on in weeks

I used to worry about the future
About my retirement
Wanted to give my kids the best
Now its just me and my spouse
In our house with our cat and dogs
Poetry is my new passion till death
Hurtling at 365 days per year
Time moves on in years

TIME WILL TELL

Three cheers for this world
Incomparable to yore
Some planned to take over the world
Stacked up arsenals of conquest
Preached racial purity
Only to wither in obscurity

Some things never change
Evil lives on
God watches in horror
As secret societies emerge
Plan to usurp His power
And singe his flowers

Time will tell
Time will tell

THE TURN, THE SEASON, THE REASON

Do you ever wonder when you will die? I do and I think
you do too.
Thank God we are made mortal,
to leave this earth go to another portal. I don't know
why people sob and feign sorrow
as if a beloved will rise again tomorrow.
When someone passes on,
It's time to go on the phone,
call for people to come to drink, eat and be merry,
because life is not a game of cat and mouse-like Tom
and Jerry.
No matter who you are, black, white
or whatever hue and colour,
we all end up silent at the parlour.

Who is he who says he be the master of another
human?
Who is she who says she be the queen among all
women?
With all riches, the time reaches when you join the food
chain
as flotsam discharged to the flood plain.

I beseech you my brothers and sisters, significant others
and all creatures,
do good unto others and your soul will rest in peace,
your tombstone we will kiss.
We will have wine, whiskey, and beer and your passing
will be our cheer,
because the laws of death are not ours,
and bury you in hours. Such is life.

WHAT A PITY

Life in the city
Has become so uncertain
Let's lift the curtain
Admit we have a problem
Who to blame?
Muggings, break-ins, and murder most foul
We might have to carry a point four four

Every evening I get home uneasy
At around eight in the evening
I scan the area around my gate
Ziggy and Flossy act as a bait
They run out and bark at any moving thing
I enjoy the scene
But I know thugs are cunning
They will wait in the car till we are coming

In Harare, we used to be free
To get drunk sleep under a tree
Walk in the dark in the park
Never worrying if you are stuck
We were the cool helpful thugs
Running the city doing drugs
The leaders who lead us
Lead us to Incubus and Succubus

Be afraid
Be very afraid
Of the new life
Thug life

THRILL AFTER THRILL

It starts with a word
That unique word in the world
It could be a noun, adjective, or verb
A collection of words turning to a verse then a reverb
Giving a thrill
Thrill after thrill

A stanza gives a picture
A glimpse, a tincture
You add detail
Shape and form like in retail
Images having a thrill
Thrill after thrill

A poem is born
Another verse clothes the bone
A life of its own
Like a rocket flown
Filling with thrill
Thrill after thrill

WIN SCORN SIN

Knight in shining armor caused no pain
Another dark demon valiantly slain
Seven slashes to back
He fell dark so black
A Win Scorn Sin hero, video so plain

Things fall apart

Things fall apart in the Land Of The Free World
What's happening to you, my word!
Why are there many contradictions?
Why do you need so many interdictions?
To stop your dark unnecessary spiral to oblivion
To stop your killing black people as a religion
Surely, one race cannot claim a monopoly,
to a nation built on immigration and oligopoly
You have built a real multi-racial society
It's why you are so strong, why the anxiety?
You have the strongest military ready to joust and win
Your enemy is not coming from abroad but is within
Your lack of choice of decisive leadership
You can lie, but the internet tells the truth to its
readership

It's great. The black background is great.
So, yes, the cover is accepted.

THERE IS A REASON I AM NOT SAD

There is a reason I am not sad
Though I live with a moody person
I am not sad because it's not bad

There is a reason I am not sad
He goes through all states of mind
I can handle it without going mad

I am not sad because it's not bad
He no longer obsesses about death,
the scriptures and verses only a tad

There is a reason I am not sad
With combinations of drugs he takes
it becomes a non-event just a fad

I am not sad because it's not bad
It's amazing the level of intelligence,
memory as sharp as a young lad

He no longer wears a special badge
No more thoughts of helplessness
I am not sad because it's not bad
There is a reason I am not sad
So, yes, the cover is accepted.
you like it. thank u
Although I think the first title should be in plain text
because it's a poetic expression...then the second can
be italicized. What do you think?

VAMPIRE STATE

Stealth in the dark
To leave a red mark
It will never heal
It will never conceal
Plasma in flood
Blood dripping in mud
You are fast asleep
Punctures just as deep
Economic losses
Tuberculosis
Immune system compromised
Platelets jeopardized
Your pulse and heart rate
Belong to the Vampire State

THE LAST OF THE SURVIVORS

Just a few of us were now left
Compassion and empathy bereft
Only one hundred metres to the ferry
The virus closing in on us with fire and fury
We had travelled from far and wide
And this was the last stretch to the ride
Maps, masks, and vaccines we threw away
These were weighing us down, we stopped even to pray

I knew I had the best chance to make it
I had slowly put antifreeze in the water left to drink
The effects were becoming obvious
The other ninety-nine in advanced degeneration
And I, though scurvy like, disheveled and smelly, had a
way of regeneration
A jerry can of good water and glucose sweets
Oh my, what manna tasting so sweet!

Every metre I crawled to the ferry a man dropped dead
Instead of helping I smiled instead
The engine of the ferry I could hear it run
And in the interminable distance a new dawn a new
rising sun
Big men and small men continued to fall and I crawl to
the boat
Egged on by the will to live and the pain in my throat
Determined was I to be the last of the survivors
To get on to the boat partake of food water and other
revivers

As I expected the last man dropped dead a metre from
the gangplank

I smiled at my prowess, having made sure the last
antifreeze he drank.
I was the last of the survivors, I felt great
I was now at the proverbial heavens gate
The cloud of pestilence closing in fast
Onto the boat every one lay dead, they didn't last
I was truly the last of the survivors in history
I sat on dead bodies laughing in delirium at my sad
story.

THE JOKE

My friend RM Smith says I m a joker
L. Tom Hankins also pulled a shocker
Seconding him in the treasonous act
So I have to prove the deed after the fact.
So I m hard-pressed to find a joke
Something, new, fresh and bespoke

The Federation of Jokers Associations has rules
To maintain standards and make sure the public is not
fooled
No lurid jokes
Unnecessary pokes
No screens for smokes
Jokes in steady strokes
No racially acidic talks
Jokes must always rock
Nothing was taken from TikTok
No jokes about dreadlocks

So here goes
Something no one knows.
"Why is five afraid of six? "
"Because seven eight nine"
I bet you are all laughing fine
Ribs cracking in pure mirth
The best joke in the world since birth
If you ever heard this joke at all
You can also laugh cause that's the joke. Thanks!

ISM ISN'T

Communism is not humanism
Capitalism is not a cataclysm
Racism is not apartheid
Fascism is not skinheads

They are isms
Ideas in prisms
People in prison
For no good reason.

Free your mind
For humankind
In the fallacies
Find balances

I know what I want
Despite the strident rant
I know what I like
I want a good life

When the firebrand stands at the podium
Whips up emotion like an isotope of Uranium Sodium
Remember history
Hysteria is not a mystery

Ism isn't
It isn't it
It isn't pleasing
Ism isn't

NEGRIL GROOVE

What happened happened
Bad very sad
Strange but won't change
The pain stain

Time crime is forgot
Work the world with bigots
Time crime is forgot
Work the world of bigots

Slavery bravery reloaded
Strength length railroaded
Move prove improve
Approve beat the groove

Time crime is forgot
Work the world of bigots
Time crime is forgot
Work the world with bigots

Improve
Move
Approve
Negril groove

A RESTING PLACE OF GOOD PEACE

A resting place of good peace
From birth, I have been looking
There in my maternal ocean
In nine evacuated
The feeding tube unceremoniously severed
Into a dangerous room full of mourning souls
Aliens dressed in white

A resting place of good peace
So-called siblings dribbling
Feigning affection
Someone called father rather
Coming hard on my viability
Mother other than suckling
Buckling to the whims of many.

A resting place of good peace
A home of my lone own
Attractions of a curvy centre
Enter the dragon, the paragon
She came conditionally upon my stroke
Bespoke tastes and preferences
Accommodation in peace entreaties

A resting place of good peace
Wherever I go told to move
The wrong ethnicity, rights denied
Like they, born with land at hand
And I, an alien without lien
The basis axes are hurled at me
Fighting to be free like on a plantation of trees.

A resting place of good peace
There
To be fair
Underwritten in sweat and blood
See how incendiary drops indiscriminately
Carnage, bandage, savage, pillage
Backed by doctored writs, and crooked books full of
gook de gook.
For a resting place of good peace.

OBRIGADO DELGADO

There is a dark slippery fluid
Deep in the bowels of the earth
If you have lived on top of it
And not known it
Big money wants it
Grant it

They sacrifice your blood to the gods of war
What's more
The scriptures spreading words of love and
togetherness
Become strictures through which your blood will flood
the slippery fluid.

Ruthless capitalists
Do not capitulate
They calculate
The B.P.D
Blood pools per day
Supplying intelligence
For intransigence

Brother fighting brother
Blaming each other
The curse of wealthiness
The case of the curse of wealthiness.
Obrigado Delgado
Obrigada El Dorado

I CAN'T COPE

This world is not my home
My thoughts not my own
Contrived, controlled

My mortgage an uncontrollable train of no gauge
Whose wheels and deals are off
Astronomic interest rates without rebates.

I need permission to breathe
Even to breed
Rulers foolers of many men

Owners of capital never capitulate
Making fresh demands for a pound of flesh
Stressing and de-stretching my life expectancy

In seven days seven letters of demand giving seven
hours to make good.
Though rude it is understood it's no good to even
brood.
Seven minutes and seven seconds to go to my seventh
haven, incarceration.

Remand demands I give up all I have and behave
according to those affording me life
Like I was born without rights to fight for my plight.

Seven seconds left, I raised my eyes from the seven
writs and was amazed at the profligacy of the
bourgeoisie.

The proletariat worse

There is no hope.
I can't cope

THE WAR

You feel defeated
Your will and enthusiasm deleted
You have not lost at all
But in your mind, you lost the war

When you fear a Black man
He is walking wearing a turban
You draw your gun
Stand your ground

He is someone's child
You label him primitively wild
You have lost your credibility
The war is your mind's incredulity

You have already lost the battle
Despite the clangour and rattle
And your judgment error
On a march to a war on terror

Call a spade a spade
The terror is a self-made
To support a behemoth bloodthirsty industry
No care for humanity and their injury

The biggest war before war
Is the mind even more
As they say "The hearts and minds"
The mind battle is the real grind

The prejudice in your mind
Hatred in your mind

The obsession in your mind
Assumptions in your mind
Gullibility in your mind
The greed in your mind
Fallibility in your mind
Superiority in your mind
Inferiority in your mind
Self-righteousness in your mind
In objectivity in your mind
Subjectivity in your mind
Feelings of grandeur in your mind
Misplaced religiosity in your mind
Disdain for science in your mind
Bending reality in your mind
Lack of contrition in your mind
Absolute decisions in your mind

I can go on and on and on
Conquer your mind on your own
The biggest war
Mother of all wars
Your mind war
The real war
The war

THAT'S ME

My life, my time, my sign, my instance in the distance
I began, I swam, with a bang, I sang
I am new, like you, that's true, I can do without you
Hug me, tug me, bug me, shrug me
See me, free me, beat me, trick me, let me be
I live, I give, I forgive, I believe, that's me.
It took no fluke, rebuke the spook, the crook, in the
Book
Lovers, my mother, my father, then brothers and
sisters, then me.

THE FORK

I came to the fork
One limb had a ford
If I crossed the river
There was the hope of a life-giver
There was hope
If I didn't drown at the ford

The second led to freedom
A new freer kingdom
I would be free to live
As long as allegiance I give
To my new oppressor
Pleasure under pressure

The third option was a loop road
Back to where I stood abroad
The safety of hindsight
The same issues I had to fight
These were my choices
In my mind my voices

I came to the fork
Each path had a yoke
A, B, or C
All I wanted was to be free.
I turned on my heels
Headed for unknown hills

FREE

Bought a cream bun
Sat in the sun
Broke my fast
The air was free

Paid my fare
Sat in my seat
Stretched my feet
The air was free

Paid my taxes
My pound of flesh
A new tax fresh
The air was free

Wherever I go
I do my prayer
To stop the slayer
The air is free

Free free free
Don't pay a fee
Free for me
The air is free

THE ANSWER IS HERE

No need to gossip
About me, close zip
Your mouth and your thoughts
Just as you were taught

It's very very simple
Never mind my dimple
If you want to know stuff
There is nothing tough

Tap me on my shoulder
Though my bicep is like a boulder
There is no risk of violence
Your safety I will not violate

So go ahead ask
It's not a hard task
Never ever fear
The answer is here

STOWAWAYS

To my dear wife
I need to improve my life
I m coming to join you
There in the EU
It can be done
It's risky and bothersome
But will be there soon
By the next afternoon
Be ready for me
Wait under the tree

I am very poor
Can't go through the door
But I have a plan
Will hide behind the turbofan
As a baggage handler
Hide myself in the hangar
In the undercarriage nook
Sorry to be a crook
I love you so
This you know

I might die of hypoxia
High altitude hypothermia
I hear many made it
I will take the risk
They call us stowaways
For you can't stay away
Meet me at the airport
Next to the airforce
If I don't make it at all
We meet at heaven's door

SUBLIMINAL MESSAGING

One day the morbidity of our lovelessness will hit its peak. Humanity looking for a place to hide.

There will be nowhere to hide

Caves will be bat-infested, they themselves the bats, carriers of viruses. SARS-COVID 19 being the most benign. Sharp canines and heparin-filled saliva to ensure you are sucked of red blood cells to the cell. To the soul. To the core.

Caves out of bounds. Bunkers debunked. Underground systems grounded. Flooded and muddied. Redundant. Defunded.

Hiding in or under a tree will be suicidal, every tree taking the brunt of electrostatic charges from clouds so contaminated with radioactive hate that only a few trees will still be standing. Standing like humans with arms skyward stretched in prayer. Answers to prayers seemingly ricocheting on steel like shrouds of tainted clouds weeping death to the earth. Crying radioactive acid rain flowing to the sea. The tree you see you flee to the sea for amelioration. But!

The sea boiling and all mountains spewing lava and ash from the deepest bowels of mother earth. The result of thermonuclear explosions deep in the core of the earth's mantle. The earth no longer the loving mother having herself been abused, raped, and rendered sterile by the hatred of one man against another. The hatred of the progeny by the progenitor. Femicide, infanticide, homicide.

The basis of the hate unfathomably obvious.

Domi-Nation. Nations of humans condemned to DamNation. Human life is priced in colourful denomiNations. Notional nomiNations of who leaves or who lives.

We see it. We have seen it already happening. A grotesque debate on who gets to live and who doesn't.

Subliminal messaging.

STREET POETRY

Am at the tyre repairman
Left front tyre separated badly
New tyres are too expense
So am getting an old one without damage extensive
From a second-hand tyre dealer
though this practice could be a killer
I look up " Tyre man Glen Norah" on my phone
Glen Norah is a High-Density suburb far from home
This is the "Ghetto" where I grew up
I know a lot of good solid guys
In Glen, Norah is where I saw the war
In nineteen seventy-nine I still recall more and more
The battle captured in my poem "War is not boring"
In nineteen seventy-nine guerillas in the city living
among us and scoring.

Glen Norah, my Ghetto, has changed a lot
I have a shop there, to live among my people, which I
bought.
To the south of Wasu, the tyre man is now a secondary
school
To the east residential houses and a community hall too
To the north of the shopping centre, my shop behind
the front row
My shop was the first to be built during Rhodesia, that I
know
To the west are residential houses and three-storey
apartments
The main road from the city passes between these with
an embarkment
The small house we lived in during the war is the fifth
from the corner

Facing the blocks of flats, in which then, lived more
affluent owners
Where the secondary school is was open bush where
we used to play
Before I finish this street poetry today just wanna say
Behind the bush towards Mukuvisi River is a small hill
On that hill one day we met guerillas with their
weaponry it was quite a thrill

The battle of Glen Norah of August nineteen seventy-
nine.
Happened between the end of residential houses and
flats at the end of the main road to town.
"War is not boring"
'Some dying others scoring"

SPOTS FULL OF DIRTY

Leopard is very selfish
Drags you through the mud
Feels justified to do this
·Feels has a right in doing this

When the other animal retaliates
Its spots full of dirty
Its spots full of dirty
Spots full of dirty

Black people were traumatized
In Azania under apartheid
In Zimbabwe under the settler regime
In the whole world under a false narrative

When the other animal retaliates
It's spots full of dirty
It's spots full of dirty
Spots full of dirty

SLAVE DRIVER

Hate them or love them
Slave drivers know the game
They get things done
Every day chasing the sun

We have made progress
People working under duress
Workers sweating under threat
Of being punished under stress

Things never happen on their own
People won't put their shoulder to the stone
Adrenaline needs a stimulus
Not just a planning calculus

When the world makes progress
We erect statues in a fortress
To commemorate dead slaves
Who died to make the haves have

It is the slave driver the conniver
credit is given to the receiver
Stop whining and pining
Let the slaver driver be shining

Don't compare
Life is not fair
Be the slave driver
Slave driver

ALBINISM

First of December twenty twenty
Traffic heavy as usual cars plenty plenty
Drove along High Glen Road in Harare going to
Avondale
Rainstorm threatening, rushing to avoid hail

In front was a bus belonging to Zimplats
One of the biggest platinum producers according to
ZimStats
There was a billboard on the back of the bus, as a poet, I
looked over
The words on the bus inspired this poem by a poem
lover

"The skin is just a cover"
"There is more to me than meets the eye"
"Building communities together"
I wish all community leaders could spread these words
about Albinism all over.

CACOPHONY OF NEGATIVITY

Hooray for Mister Al Gore
He said it and I wanna say it more
Thank God for the internet
Including WIFI and the intranet
You don't need to be alone
You can use your phone
Surf the wide world web
And not be lied to and misled
The dictator can't dictate
That would be a big mistake
In minutes the world will know
and have a voice, a choice to say no
Biological agents can't be discharged
The WHO will have someone charged
Africa will never be behind in tech,
never be a playground for crystal meth
Uncle Sam will not shoot Afro Americans
Then tell us about Anglo Americans.
How do you care about Afro Africans?
When you don't, your Afro Americans
Three cheers for Mister Al Gore
We love you, Sir, Mrs. Gore all the more

JAH RUINS

There is a hill in Glen Norah
next to my mother's house.
The hill is the centre of religion.
The Apostolic Faith people
meet there.
The Christians meet there
for open-air worship.
The Rastafarian brethren
built their temple at the top.
A temple made of rocks piled up.

I used to sit at the summit of the hill.
From the top, you see the school
called Glen Norah Infill.
You see people toiling
on their maize fields.
You see lovers walking hand in hand.
You see the splendour of creation.
Birds sing hymns you
never heard of before.

The hill is called Jah Ruins.
The hill is called Jah Ruins.
Reminds me of the Great Zimbabwe Ruins.
We don't unite, our country is in ruins.

ABOUT THE AUTHOR

DELUKE MUWANIGWA

I am just an average guy observing the world. The miseducation of the people. The prejudices were resultant from this sustained miseducation and the toll it takes on the peace and security of the world. Being a hands-on type of person I ask myself what I can do, in my small way, to try to reverse the negativity. Being an engineer, I write a poem. Enjoy my poems. I am a Zimbabwe Engineer by profession, a poet by induction, and a father of two grown adult kids, Dananayi and Mudiwa Nathasia. Born June 18, 1964, and seen what I have seen. Experienced what I experienced. The bulk of my life I spent with my wife facing the knife and strife, it's like my ribs were taken from her to fashion my breathing allowing me to breed. There are more rhymes and alliteration in this book. Welcome to my Africa.